ALL TIME AND OLD TIME

FAVOURITES

SING OUT"

A PROJECT BY

THE SENIORS AT MARKHAVEN INC., 54 PARKWAY AVE., MARKHAM, ONTARIO L3P 2G4

Printed in U.S.A.

GORDON V. THOMPSON MUSIC

First Edition, 1973

In 1970 the Ontario government prepared a book of All Time and Old Time Favourites to be available to all Senior Citizen Homes, Clubs and Centres, and adult Charitable Institutions for use by the members, residents, auxiliaries and staff.

But these contained words only. So in 1973 our group applied and were awarded a New Horizons Grant to produce a music book to go along with the words. We pitched the songs a little lower, in a key that is easier for seniors to sing. The type is easy to read, and the arrangements are simple enough for most pianists to be able to sit down and play.

We are grateful to the residents of the various Senior Citizen Homes who worked with us on this project.

Without the unstinting co-operation of the many music companies holding the copyrights on the selections included, we could never have gone to press. We thank them for their help and good wishes in joining with us to bring joy through music into the lives of seniors in the Province of Ontario.

We hope you enjoy.

Markhaven "SING OUT" Committee:

Elgin Thomson, President
George G. Grose, Treasurer
Eva M. Cottom, Secretary

Emily Busby	Mable Grose
Winnifred Hyde	Mary Rose
Florence Mear	Cora Seymour
Louisa Patterson	Mabel Gill
Betty Warren	Agnes Wharrad
Mary Dyson	Pear Scott
Ida Richardson	Helen Stephenson
Leslie Hyde	Elsie Warmoll

Second Edition, 1976-77

The Senior Citizens' Branch — Office on Aging was pleased in 1976 to assist Markhaven in printing this music book. Now due to popular demand, we are providing funds for a Second Edition, as well as reprinting the Sixth Edition of our large-print "Sing Out" for Senior Citizens in Ontario. We are especially grateful to Mrs. Lois Neeley, Administrator, Markhaven, for her efforts in distributing this further supply of the music, and to her associates at Markhaven, for their earlier work.

Information regarding the publications or other matters relating to seniors, please contact:

Office for Senior Citizens Affairs
76 College Street, 6th Floor
Queen's Park
Toronto, Ontario M7A 1N3
Telephone (416) 327-2422. Collect calls are accepted within Ontario.

I Dream of Jeanie
with the Light Brown Hair

STEPHEN C. FOSTER

2

Good-night, Ladies

COLLEGE SONG

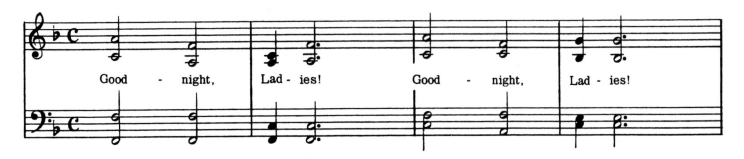

Good - night, Lad - ies! Good - night, Lad - ies!

Good - night, Lad - ies! We're going to leave you now.

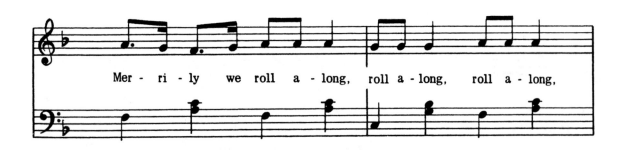

Mer - ri - ly we roll a - long, roll a - long, roll a - long,

Mer - ri - ly we roll a - long, o'er the deep blue sea.

Aura Lee

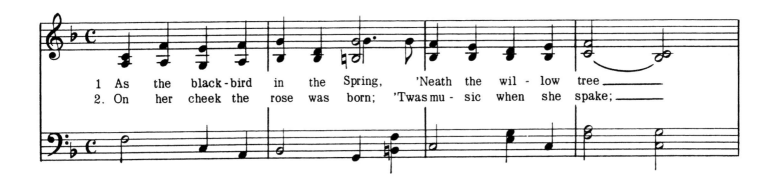

1 As the black-bird in the Spring, 'Neath the wil - low tree_____
2. On her cheek the rose was born; 'Twas mu - sic when she spake;_____

Sat and piped, I heard him sing, Sing - ing Au - ra Lee.
In her eyes the rays of morn, With sud - den splen-dour break.

Au - ra Lee, Au - ra Lee Maid with gold - en hair
Au - ra Lee, Au - ra Lee Maid with gold - en hair

Sun - shine came a - long with thee, And swal - lows in the air.
Sun - shine came a - long with thee, And swal - lows in the air.

4   Anniversary Song

AL JOLSON and SAUL CHAPLIN

Oh, _____ how we danced, _____ on the night _____

_____ we were wed. _____ We vowed _____ our true

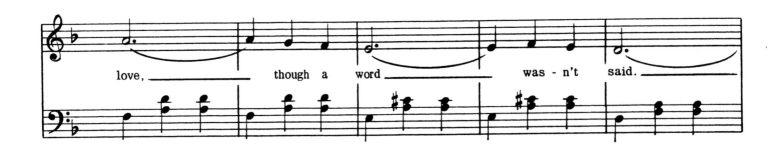

love, _____ though a word _____ was - n't said. _____

_____ The world _____ was in bloom, _____ there were

stars _____ in the skies, _____ Ex - cept _____ for the

few _____ that were there _____ in your eyes. _____

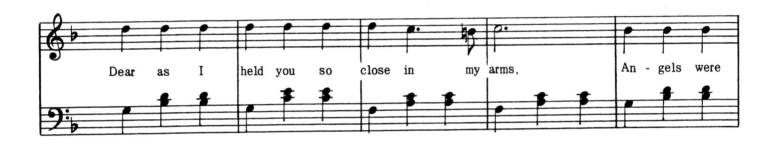

Dear as I held you so close in my arms, An - gels were

sing - ing a hymn to your charms. Two hearts gent - ly beat - ing were

mur - mur - ing low, "My dar - ling, I love you so." _____

5 All the Nice Girls Love a Sailor

A.J.MILLS

BENNETT SCOTT

6   Easter Parade

IRVING BERLIN

In your East - er bon - net, With all the frills up -

on it, You'll be the grand - est la - dy in the

East - er Par - ade. I'll be all in clov - er: And

when they look you ov - er, I'll be the proud - est fel - low in the

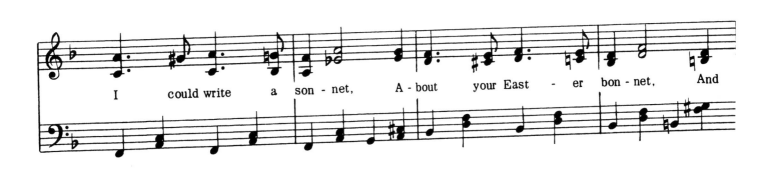

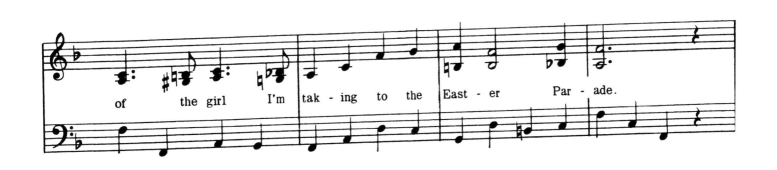

When You're Smiling

MARK FISHER, JOE GOODWIN and LARRY SHAY

When you're smil - ing, _____ when you're smil - ing, _____

The whole world smiles with you; _____

When you're laugh - ing, _____ when you're laugh - ing, _____

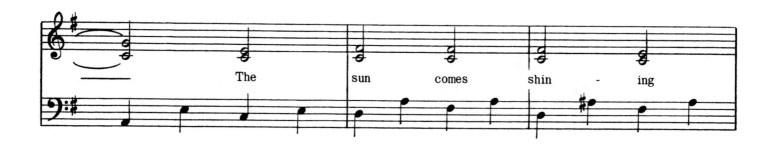

The sun comes shin - ing

8 In the Shade of the Old Apple Tree

HARRY WILLIAMS

EGBERT VAN ALSTYNE

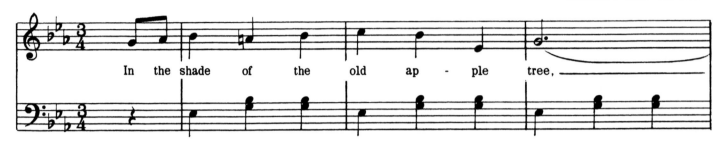

In the shade of the old ap - ple tree, ____

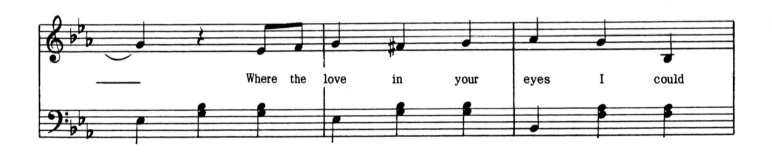

Where the love in your eyes I could

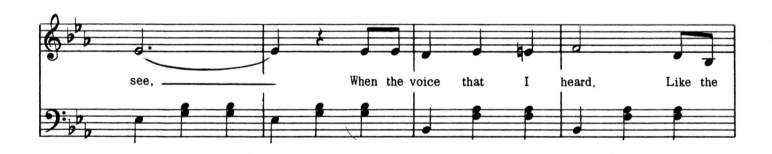

see, ____ When the voice that I heard, Like the

song of the bird, Seem'd to whis - per sweet

9   I Want to Be Happy

IRVING CAESAR

VINCENT YOUMANS

I want to be hap - py, But I won't be hap - py

Till I make you hap - py, too. _____

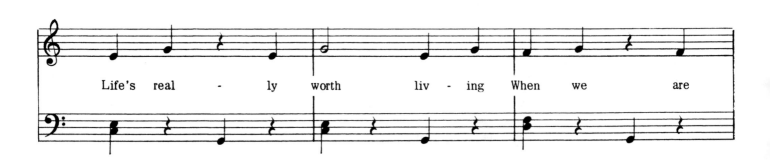

Life's real - ly worth liv - ing When we are

mirth giv - ing, Why can't I give some to

10 Shine on Harvest Moon

NORA BAYES and JACK NORWORTH

11 Side by Side

HARRY WOODS

Oh, we ain't got a bar-rel of mon-ey May-be we're rag-ged and fun-ny, But we'll trav-el a-long, ___ sing-ing a song, ___ Side by side. We don't know what's com-ing to-mor-row, May-be it's trou-ble and sor-row, But we'll trav-el the road, ___ shar-ing the load, ___ Side by

side. In all kinds of weath - er, — What if the sky should

fall, As long as we're to - geth - er, It does - n't mat - ter at

all. When they've all had their trou-bles and part - ed, We'll be the same as we

start - ed, Just trav-el-in' a - long, — sing-in' a song, —

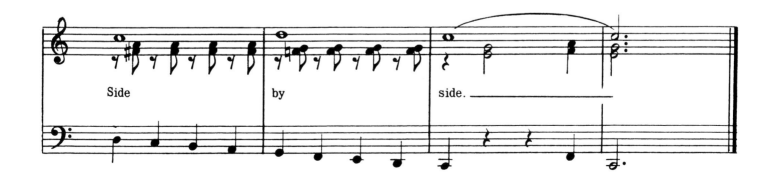

Side by side. _____

12 Smiles

J. WILL CALLAHAN

LEE S. ROBERTS

There are smiles _____ that make us hap - py, _____

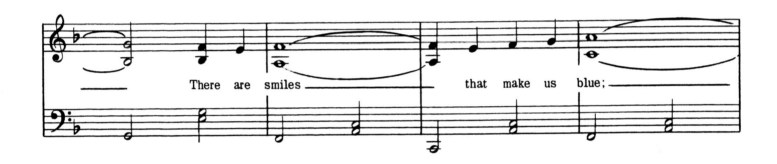

_____ There are smiles _____ that make us blue;

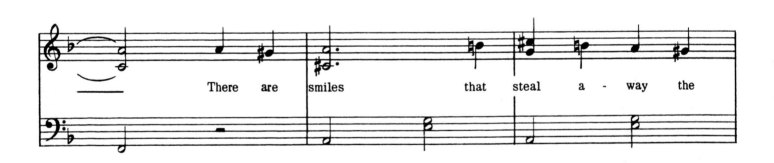

_____ There are smiles that steal a - way the

tear - drops _____ As the sun - shine steals a - way the

dew: _____ There are smiles that have a ten - der

mean - ing, _____ That the eyes of love a - lone may

see, _____ But the smiles that

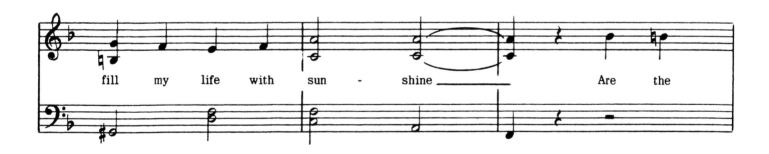

fill my life with sun - shine _____ Are the

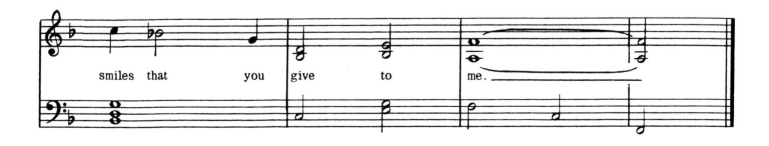

smiles that you give to me. _____

13 You're the Cream in My Coffee

B.G. DESYLVA, LEW BROWN and RAY HENDERSON

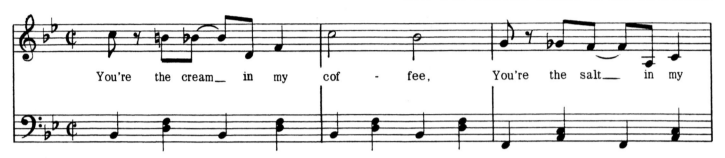

You're the cream__ in my cof - fee, You're the salt__ in my

stew. You wil al - ways be my ne -ces -si -ty, I'd be lost__ with-out

you. You're the starch in my col - lar, You're the lace__ in my

shoe. You will al - ways be my ne - ces - si - ty,

I'd be lost _ with - out you. Most men _ tell love - tales _

And each _ phrase dove - tails. _ You've heard _ each

known way, This way _ is _ my own _ way.

You're the sail _ of my love - boat, You're the cap - tain and crew,

You will al - ways be my ne - ces - si - ty I'd be lost _ with - out you.

14   If You Were the Only Girl

CLIFFORD GREY

NAT D. AYER

If you were the on - ly girl in the world, And I was the on - ly boy, _____

No - thing else would mat - ter in the world to - day,

We could go on lov - ing in the same old way — A gar - den of

15 I've Got a Luverly Bunch of Coconuts

FRED HEATHERTON

I've got a luv-er-ly bunch of co - co -nuts,

There they are, a - stand -ing in a row; Big ones, small ones,

some as big as yer 'ead, Give 'em a twist, a flick of the wrist, That's

what the show-man said. He said: I've got a luv-er -ly bunch of co - co -nuts;

Ev - e -ry ball I throw will make me rich,

There stands me wife, _____ the i - dol of me life, Sing - ing

Roll - a - bowl - a - ball - a - pen-ny - a - pitch! _____ Sing - ing, Roll - a - bowl - a -

ball - a - pen-ny - a - pitch! _____ Sing - ing, Roll - a - bowl - a - ball - a - pen - ny - a

pitch! _____ Roll - a - bowl - a - ball! Roll - a - bowl - a

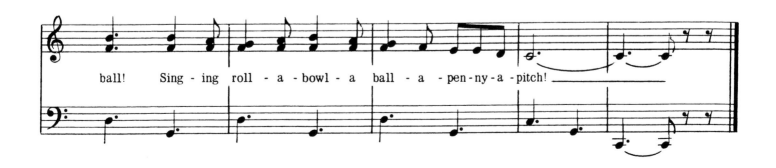

ball! Sing - ing roll - a - bowl - a ball - a - pen-ny - a - pitch! _____

16   Zip-a-dee-doo-dah

RAY GILBERT

ALLIE WRUBEI

Zip - A - Dee - Doo - Dah, Zip - A - Dee - Ay,___

My, oh my___ what a won-der-ful day!

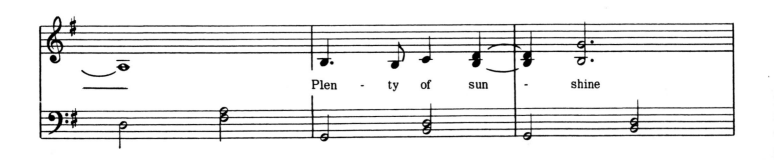

Plen - ty of sun - shine

head - ing my way.___ Zip - A - Dee - Doo - Dah,

Zip - A - Dee - Ay, _____ There's a blue - bird

on my shoul - der, _____ It's the truth, it's

"at - ch'll," Ev - 'ry - thing is "sat - is fact - ch'll,"

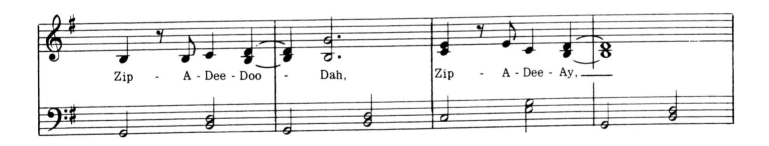

Zip - A - Dee - Doo - Dah, Zip - A - Dee - Ay, _____

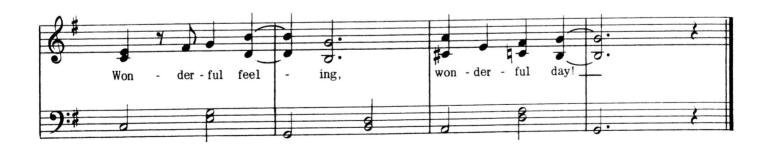

Won - der - ful feel - ing, won - der - ful day! _____

17   Five Foot Two, Eyes of Blue

SAM LEWIS and JOE YOUNG

RAY HENDERSON

Five foot two, __ eyes of blue __ But oh, what those __ five

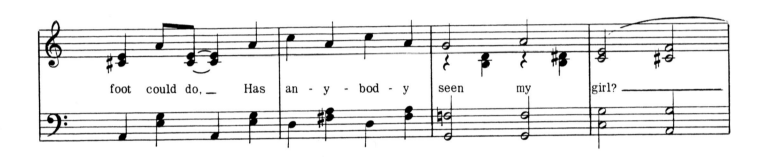

foot could do, __ Has an - y - bod - y seen my girl? _____

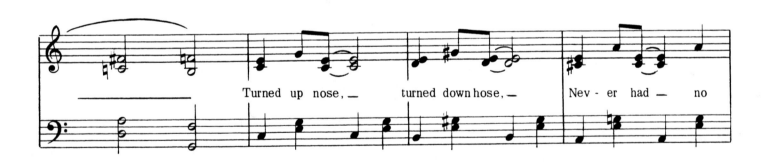

_____ Turned up nose, __ turned down hose, __ Nev - er had __ no

oth - er beaus, __ Has an - y - bod - y seen my girl? _____

Now if you run in-to a five foot two,—

Cov - ered with fur, Dia - mond rings and all those things,

Bet - cha life it is - n't her,— But could she love,—

could she woo?— Could she, could— she, could she coo?— Has

an - y - bod - y seen my girl? _____

18 Billy Boy

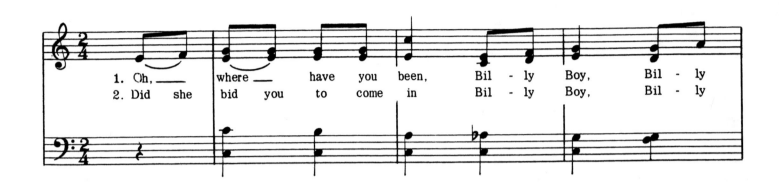

1. Oh,___ where ___ have you been, Bil - ly Boy, Bil - ly
2. Did she bid you to come in Bil - ly Boy, Bil - ly

Boy, Oh, ___ where ___ have you been, charm - ing Bil - ly?
Boy, Did she bid you to come in charm - ing Bil - ly?

I have been to seek a wife, She's the joy ___ of my
Yes, she bade me to come in, There's a dim - ple on her

life, She's a young thing and can - not leave her moth - er. ___
chin, She's a young thing and can - not leave her moth - er. ___

19 April Showers

B.G. DESYLVA

LOUIS SILVERS

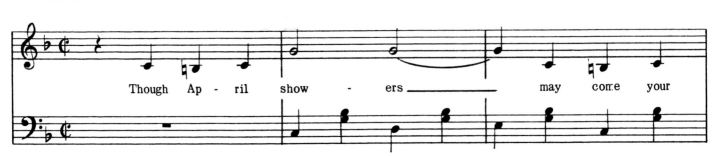

Though Ap - ril show - ers _____ may come your

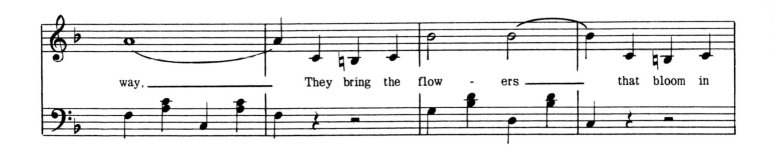

way, _____ They bring the flow - ers _____ that bloom in

May, _____ So if it's rain - ing, _____ have no re -

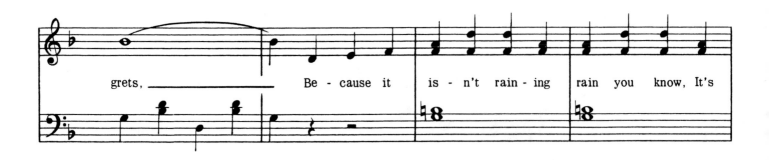

grets, _____ Be - cause it is - n't rain - ing rain you know, It's

rain - ing vi - o - lets. And when you see clouds _____

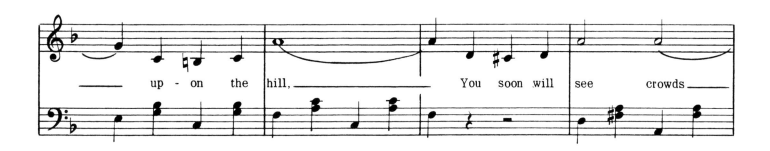

_____ up - on the hill, _____ You soon will see crowds _____

_____ of daf - fo - dils, _____ So keep on look - ing for a

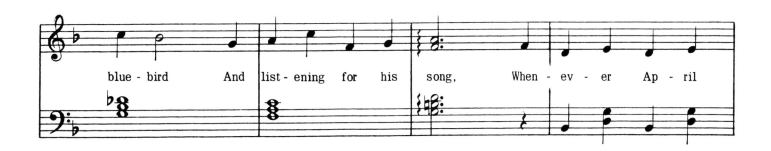

blue - bird And list - en - ing for his song, When - ev - er Ap - ril

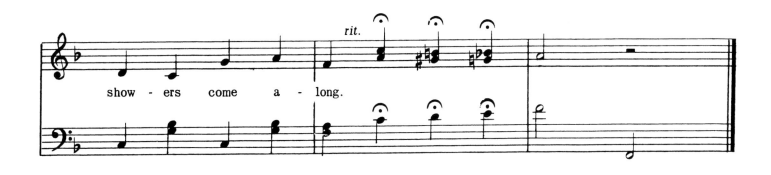

rit.

show - ers come a - long.

20   I've Got Sixpence

Words and Music by COX, BOX and HALL

I've got six - pence, jol - ly, jol - ly six - pence, I've got six - pence to

last me all my life. I've got tup - pence to spend and tup - pence to lend And

tup - pence to send home to my wife, poor wife. No __ cares have I to

grieve _____ me, No pret - ty lit - tle girls to de - cei - ve me. I'm

hap - py as a king, be - lie - ve me, As we go rol - ling, rol - ling

home. Rol - ling home, (Rol - ling home) Rol - ling home, (Rol - ling home) By the

light of the sil - ver - y moon. _____ Hap - py is the day when a

sold - ier gets his pay As we go rol - ling, rol - ling home.

21 Clementine

P. MONTROSE

In a cav - ern, by a can - yon, Ex - ca -

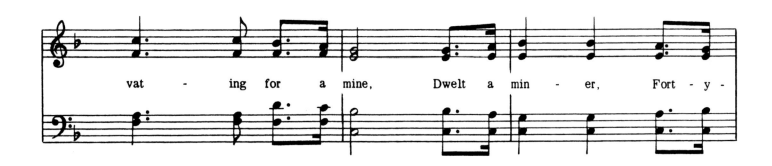

vat - ing for a mine, Dwelt a min - er, Fort - y -

ni - ner, And his daugh - ter, Clem - en - tine.

CHORUS

Oh, my dar - ling, Oh, my dar - ling, Oh, my

dar - ling Clem - en - tine, Thou are lost and gone for -

ev - er, Dread - ful sor - ry, Clem - en - tine.

2. Light she was and like a fairy,
   And her shoes were number nine,
   Herring boxes without topses.
   Sandals were for Clementine.

3. Drove her ducklings to the water
   Every morning just at nine,
   Stuck her foot against a splinter,
   Fell into the foaming brine.

Beer Barrel Polka

Based on the European
success "SKODA LASKY"*

LEW BROWN, WLADIMIR A. TIMM and JAROMIR VEJVODA

There's a gar - den, what a gar - den On - ly hap - py fac - es bloom there, And there's

nev - er an - y room there for a wor - ry or a gloom there. Oh, there's

mus - ic and there's dan - cing And a lot of sweet ro - man - cing.

When they play a pol - ka They all get in the swing. Ev - 'ry

time they hear that oom - pa - pa Ev - 'ry -
hear a rum - ble on the floor; It's the

Roll out the bar - rel

We've got the blues on the run. Zing!

Boom! Tar - ar - rel! Ring out a song of good

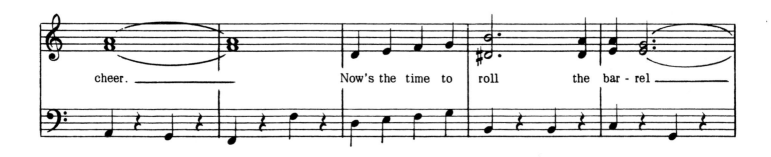

cheer. Now's the time to roll the bar - rel

For the gang's all here.

Lilli Marlene

NORBERT SCHULTZ, HANS LEIP and TOMMY CONNOR

1. Un - der-neath the lan - tern by the bar -rack gate, Darl - ing I re - mem ! ber the
2. Time would come for roll call, time for us to part. Darl - ing I'd car - ess you and
3. Ord - ers came for sail - ing, some-where o - ver there, All con -fined to bar - acks was
4. Rest - ing in a bil - let just be-hind the line, Ev - en tho' we're part - ed your

way you used to wait; 'Twas there that you whisp - ered ten - der - ly, That
press you to my heart. And there 'neath that far off lan - tern light, I'd
more than I could bear; I knew you were wait - ing in the street, I
lips are close to mine; You wait where that lan - tern soft - ly gleams, Your

you loved me, you'd al - ways be, My Lil - li of the
hold you tight, we'd kiss good - night, My Lil - li of the
heard your feet, but could not meet; My Lil - li of the
sweet face seems to haunt my dreams, My Lil - li of the

Lamp - light, My own Lil - li Mar - lene.
Lamp - light, My own Lil - li Mar - lene.
Lamp - light, My own Lil - li Mar - lene.
Lamp - light, My own Lil - li Mar - lene.

24   Mockin' Bird Hill

VAUGHN HORTON

When the sun in the morn - in' peeps ov - er the

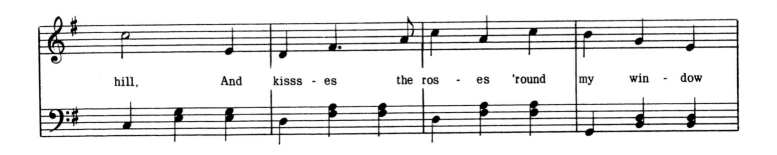

hill, And kisss - es the ros - es 'round my win - dow

sill; Then my heart fills with glad - ness when I hear the

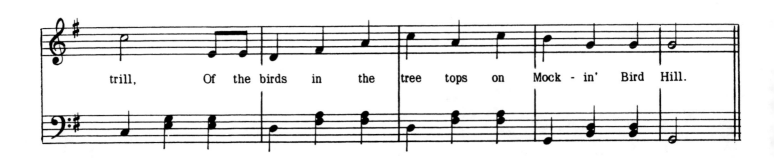

trill, Of the birds in the tree tops on Mock - in' Bird Hill.

CHORUS

Tra - la - la twit-tle-dee-dee-dee It gives me a thrill, To wake up in the morn-in' to the Mock-in' birds trill; Tra-la-la twit-tle-dee-dee-dee There's peace and good-will; You're wel-come as the flow-ers On Mock-in' Bird Hill.

1, 2   3.
2. Got a   Hill.
3. When it's

2. Got a three-cornered plow and an acre to till
   And a mule that I bought for a ten dollar bill;
   There's a tumble-down shack and a rusty old mill,
   But it's my home sweet home up on Mockin' Bird Hill.

3. When it's late in the evening, I climb up the hill
   And survey my kingdom while everything's still;
   Only me and the sky and an old whip-poor-will,
   Sing-in' songs in the twilight on Mockin' Bird Hill.

25 Red Sails in the Sunset

JIMMY KENNEDY

HUGH WILLIAMS

Red sails in the sun - set, 'Way out on the

sea, Oh! Car - ry my loved one Home safe - ly to

me. He sailed at the dawn - ing, All day I've been

blue. Red sails in the sun - set. I'm trust - ing in

you.   Swift   wings you must bor - row,   Make straight for   the

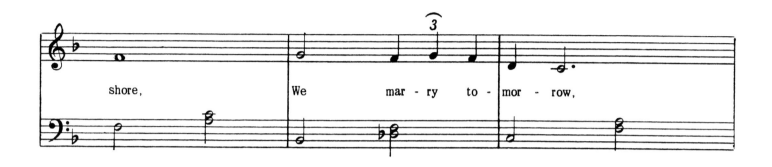

shore,   We   mar - ry to - mor - row,

And   he   goes sail - ing   no   more;   Red   sails in   the

sun - set,   'Way   out   on   the sea,   Oh!   Car - ry   my

loved   one,   Home safe - ly to   me.

26   Now is the Hour

MAEWA KAIHAN, CLEMENT SCOTT and DOROTHY STEWART

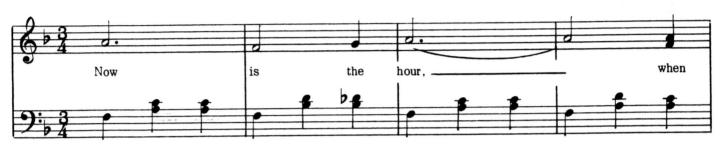

Now is the hour, _____ when

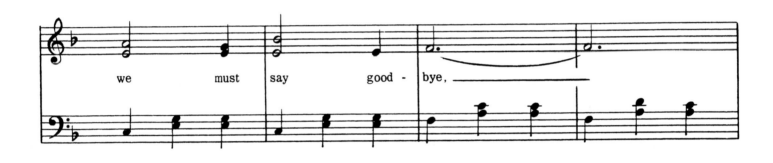

we must say good - bye, _____

Soon you'll be sail - ing

far a - cross the sea, _____

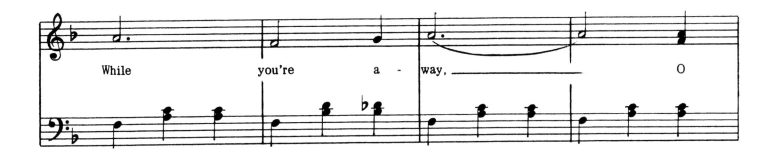

While   you're   a -   way, _____   O

then   re -   mem -   ber   me; _____

When   you   re - turn,   you'll   find   me

wait -   ing   here. _____

27 Oh Dear! What Can the Matter Be

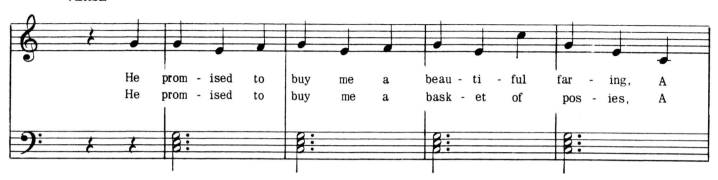

He prom - ised to buy me a beau - ti - ful far - ing, A
He prom - ised to buy me a bask - et of pos - ies, A

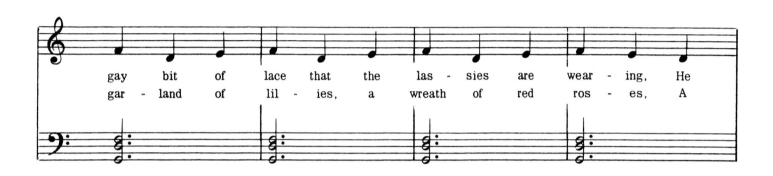

gay bit of lace that the las - sies are wear - ing, He
gar - land of lil - ies, a wreath of red ros - es, A

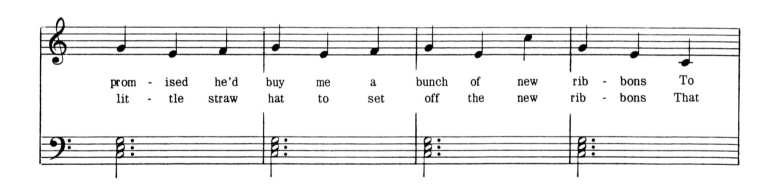

prom - ised he'd buy me a bunch of new rib - bons To
lit - tle straw hat to set off the new rib - bons That

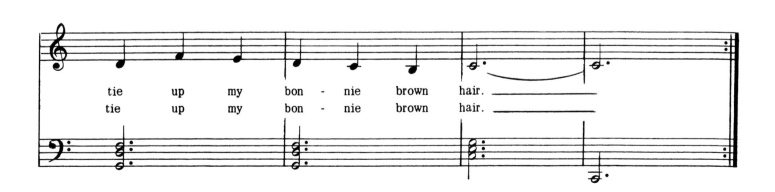

tie up my bon - nie brown hair. _____
tie up my bon - nie brown hair. _____

28 Tipperary

JACK JUDGE and HARRY WILLIAMS

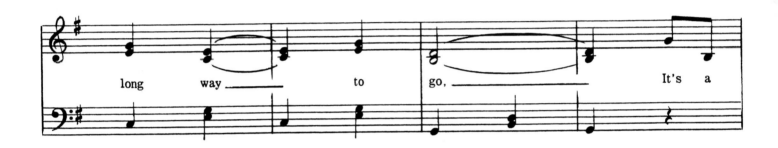

It's a long way ___ to Tip - per - a - ry ___ It's a

long way ___ to go, ___ It's a

long way ___ to Tip - per - a - ry ___ To the

sweet - est girl I know. ___

Good - bye _____ Pic - ca - dil - ly, _____

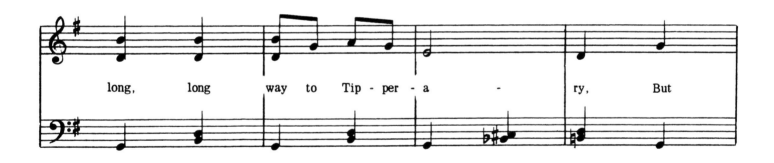

Fare - well Leices - ter Square. _____ It's a

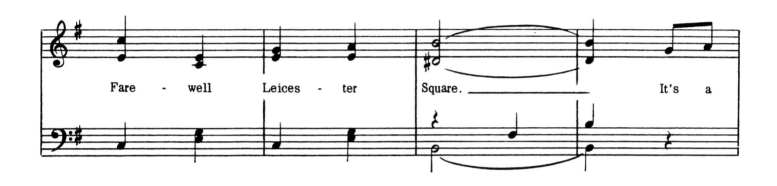

long, long way to Tip - per - a - ry, But

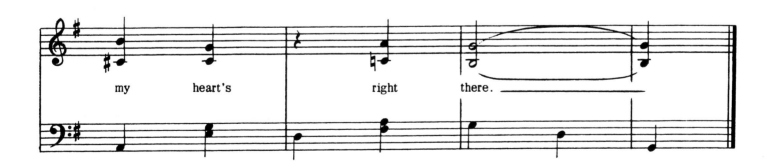

my heart's right there. _____

The Happy Wanderer

WE REGRET THAT WE WERE UNABLE TO OBTAIN THE COPYRIGHT
PRIVILEGES NECESSARY TO PRINT "THE HAPPY WANDERER".
We suggest the key of B flat, starting on F.

Harrigan, That's Me

GEORGE M. COHAN

31   Paddlin' Madelin' Home

HARRY WOODS

'Cause when I'm pa - dd -lin' Ma - de lin' home, _____ Gee! When I'm

pa - dd - lin' Ma - de - lin' home, _____ First I

drift with the tide _____ Then pull for the shore_____ I

hug her and kiss_____ her And pad - dle some more. _____ Then I keep

pa - dd - li' Ma - de - lin' home, _____ Un - til I

find a spot where ___ we're a - lone. _____ Oh! She

nev - er says "no" ___ so I kiss her and go, ___

Pad - dd - lin' Ma - de - lin', Sweet, sweet Ma - de lin',

Pa - dd - lin' Ma - de - lin home!   'Cause when I'm   home. _____

32 In a Shanty in Old Shanty Town

JOE YOUNG

LITTLE JACK LITTLE and JOHN SIRAS

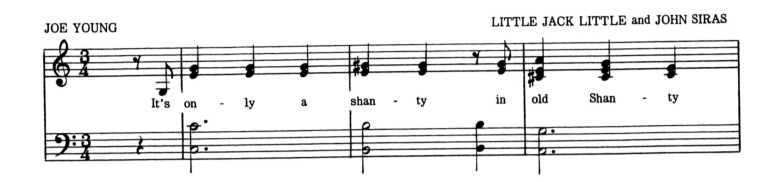

It's on - ly a shan - ty in old Shan - ty

Town, _____ The roof is so slan - ty it touch - es the

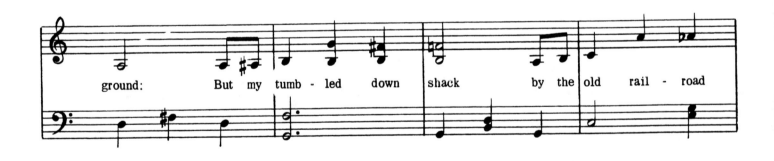

ground: But my tumb - led down shack by the old rail - road

track Like a mill - ion - aire's man - sion is call - ing me

back. _____ I'd give up a pal - ace if I were a

king; _____ It's more than a pal - ace, it's my ev - 'ry -

thing. There's a queen wait - ing there with a sil - ver - y

crown In a shan - ty in old Shan - ty Town.

33   Gimme a Little Kiss

ROY TURK, JACK SMITH and MACEO PINKARD

Gim-me a lit-tle kiss,— Will ya, huh?— What are ya gon-na miss,

Will ya, huh?— Gosh! Oh, gee! Why do you re-fuse?

I can't see what you've got to lose,— Gim-me a lit-tle squeeze,—

Will ya, huh?— Why do you wan-na make me blue, I

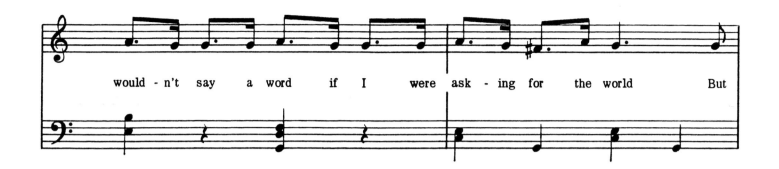

would - n't say a word if I were ask - ing for the world   But

what's a lit - tle kiss Be - tween a fel - low and his girl? So, gim - me a lit - tle kiss___

will ya huh?__ And I'll give it right back__ to you.

34 Road to Mandalay

Words by
RUDYARD KIPLING

Music by
OLEY SPEAKS

Come you back to Man - da - lay Where the old flo - til - la lay, Can't you 'ear their pad - dles chun -kin' From Ran - goon to Man - da - lay? On the road to Man - da - lay ___ Where the fly - ing fish - es play, ___ And the dawn comes up like thun-der Out of Chi - na 'cross the bay.

35 Silver Threads Among the Gold

EBEN E. REXFORD

H. P. DANKS

Dar - ling I am grow-ing old, _____ Sil - ver threads a - mong the

gold, Shine up-on my brow to - day, _____ Life is fad -ing fast a -

way, But my dar - ling you will be, (will be)

Al - ways young and fair to me, Yes! my dar -ling you will be, _____

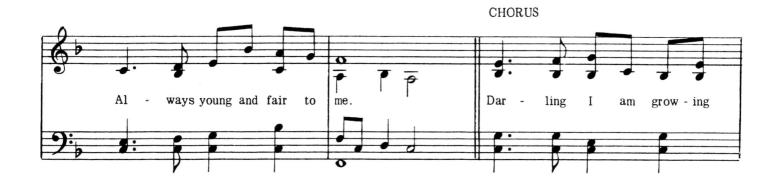

Al - ways young and fair to me. Dar - ling I am grow - ing

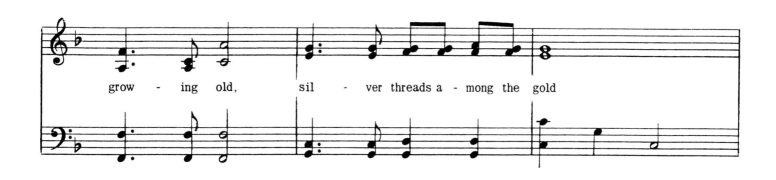

grow - ing old, sil - ver threads a - mong the gold

Shine up - on my brow to - day:_____ Life is fad - ing fast a - way.

36   Marching Along Together

English lyrics by MORT DIXON

Words and Music by EDWARD POLA
and FRANZ STEININGER

March - ing a - long _____ to - geth - er,

Shar - ing ev - 'ry smile and tear. _____ March - ing a - long _____

_____ to - geth - er, Whist - ling till the

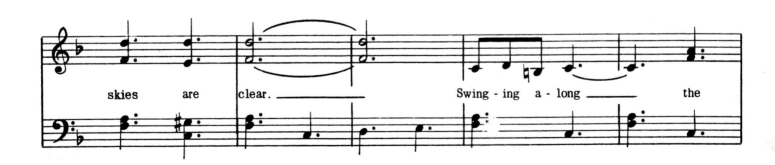

skies are clear. _____ Swing - ing a - long _____ the

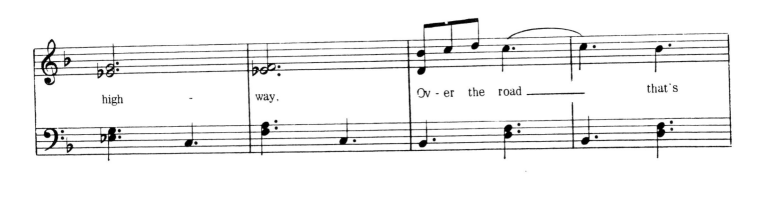

high - way, Over the road _____ that's

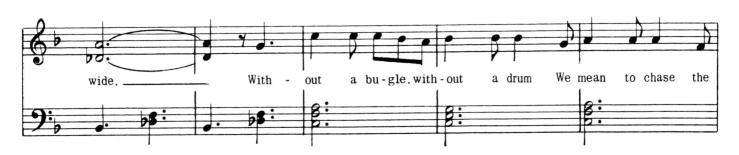

wide, _____ With - out a bu - gle, with - out a drum We mean to chase the

jinx. _____ Oh rum - ti - did - dle - di here we come, We're hap - py hin - key

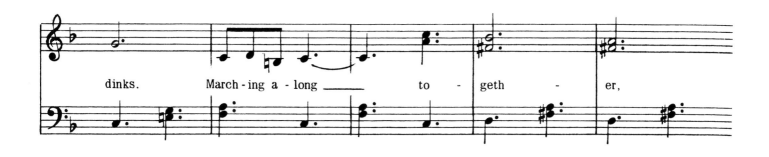

dinks. March - ing a - long _____ to - geth - er,

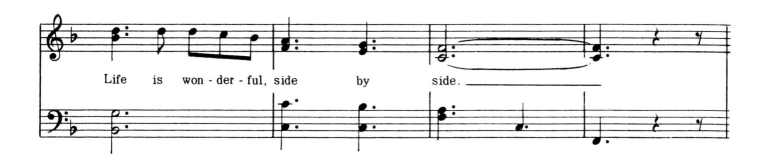

Life is won - der - ful, side by side. _____

37 Margie

BENNY DAVIS

CON CONRAD and J. RUSSEL ROBINSON

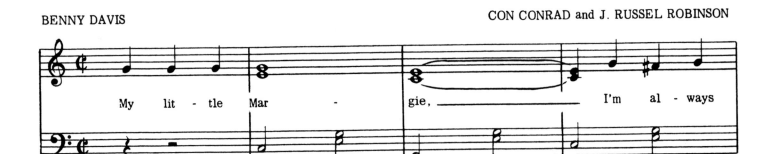

My lit - tle Mar - gie, _____ I'm al - ways

think - ing of you, Mar - gie, _____ I'll tell the

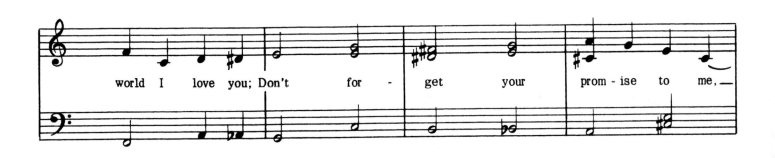

world I love you; Don't for - get your prom - ise to me, __

I have bought a home and ring and

ev - 'ry - thing, For Mar - gie, _____ you've been my

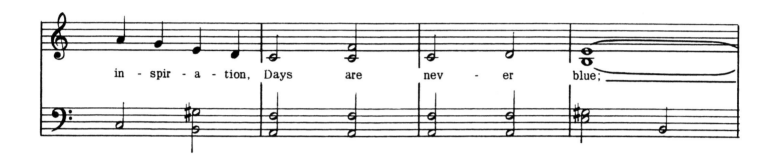

in - spir - a - tion, Days are nev - er blue; _____

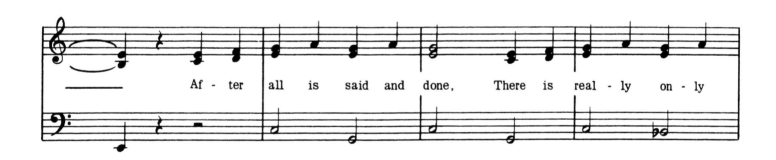

_____ Af - ter all is said and done, There is real - ly on - ly

one, Oh! Mar - gie, Mar - gie, it's you. _____

38   Home Sweet Home

JOHN HOWARD PAYNE

SIR HENRY R. BISHOP

'Mid pleas - ures and pal - ac - es though _____ we may

roam,   Be it ev - er so hum - ble, there's

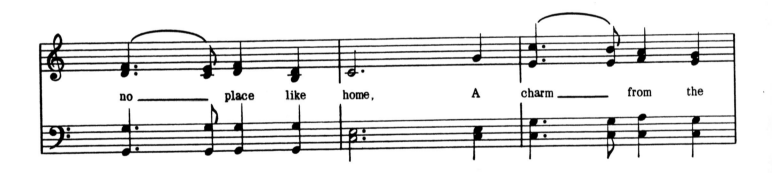

no _____ place like home,   A charm _____ from the

skies   seems to hal - low us there,   Which

seek _____ through the world, _____ is ne'er met with else - where.

CHORUS

Home, home, _____ sweet, sweet home, There's

no _____ place like home, _____ There's no _____ place like home.

39 Springtime in the Rockies

MARY HALE WOOLSEY

ROBERT SAUER

When it's spring - time in the Rock - ies ____

____ I'll be com - ing back to you. ____

____ Lit - tle sweet - heart of the moun - tains,

With your bon - nie eyes of blue. ____

Once a - gain I'll say I love you, _____

_____ While the birds sing all the day, _____

_____ When it's spring - time in the Rock - ies,

In the Rock - ies far a - way. _____

40   Harbour Lights

JIMMY KENNEDY

HUGH WILLIAMS

I saw the har - bour lights,   They on - ly told me we were part - ing,

The same old har - bour lights,   That once brought you to me.

I watched the har - bour lights,   How could I help if tears were start - ing?

Good - bye to ten - der nights   Be - side the silv - 'ry

sea. _____ I longed to hold you near And kiss you just once

more, _____ But you were on the ship And I was on the

shore. _____ Now I know lone - ly nights,

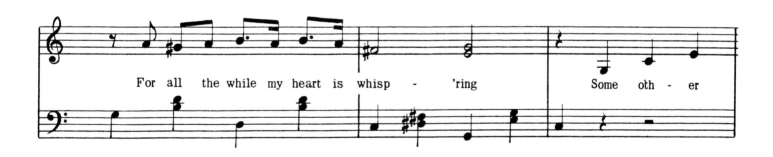

For all the while my heart is whisp - 'ring Some oth - er

har - bour lights Will steal your love from me. _____

41 Till We Meet Again

RAYMOND B. EGAN

RICHARD A. WHITING

Smile the while you kiss me sad a - dieu,

When the clouds roll by I'll come to you.

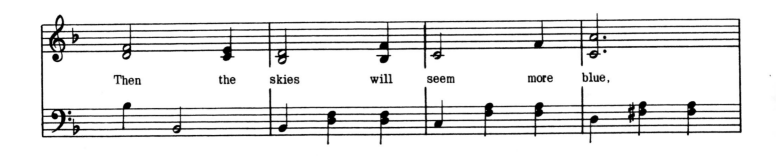

Then the skies will seem more blue,

Down in lov - ers lane, my dear - ie,

Wed - ding bells will ring so mer-ri-ly,

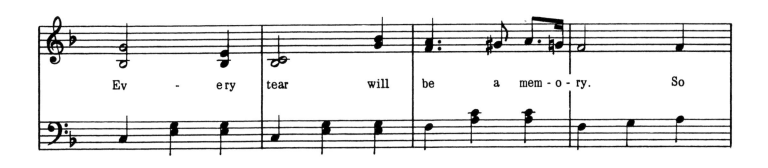

Ev - e ry tear will be a mem-o-ry. So

wait and pray each night for me,

Till we meet a - gain. _____

42   The Man on the Flying Trapeze

Oh, once I was hap-py but now I'm for-lorn, Just like an old

coat that is tat-tered and torn, I'm left in this wild world to

cry and to mourn, Be-trayed by a maid in her teens.

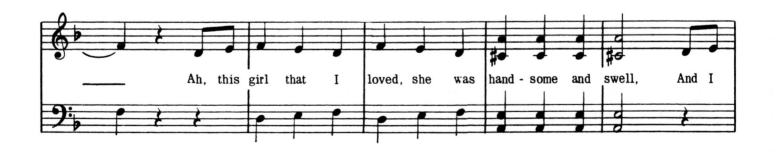

Ah, this girl that I loved, she was hand-some and swell, And I

tried all I knew her to please, _____ But I nev - er could please her one

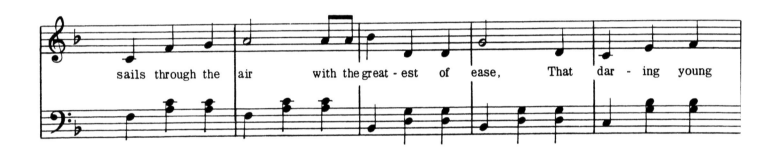

frac - tion so well As that man on the fly - ing trap - eze. Oh He

sails through the air with the great - est of ease, That dar - ing young

man on the fly - ing trap - eze; His man - ner is grace - ful, all

girls he does please, And my love he has stol - en a - way. _____

43 The Band Played On

JOHN F. PALMER

CHARLES B. WARD

Cas - ey would waltz with a straw - ber - ry blonde, And the

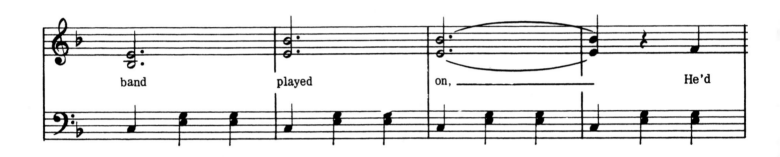

band played on, _____ He'd

glide 'cross the floor with the girl he ad - ored, And the

band played on. _____ But his

brain was so load - ed it near - ly ex - plod - ed, The

poor girl would shake with al - arm. _____ He'd

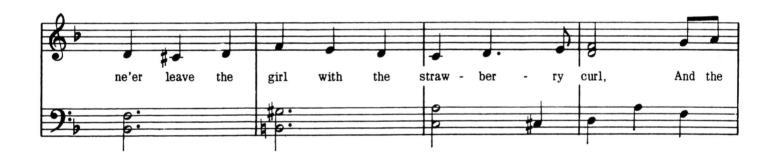

ne'er leave the girl with the straw - ber - ry curl, And the

band played on. _____

44 There's a Long, Long Trail

STODDARD KING

ZO ELLIOT

There's a long, long trail a - wind - ing, In - to the land of my dreams, Where the night - in - gales are sing - ing and a white moon beams. There's a long, long night of wait - ing, Un - til my dreams all come true, Till the day when I'll be go - ing down That long, long trail with you.

45 Let Me Call You Sweetheart

BETH SLATER WITSON

LEO FRIEDMAN

Let me call you "sweet - heart", I'm in

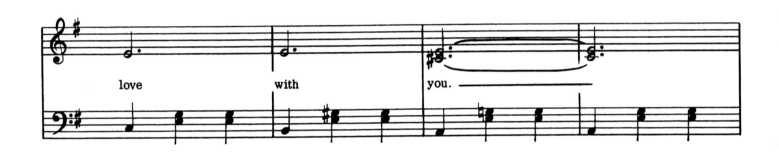

love with you. _____

Let me hear you whisp - er that you

love me, too. _____

Keep   the   love - light glow - ing   In   your

eyes   so   true; _____

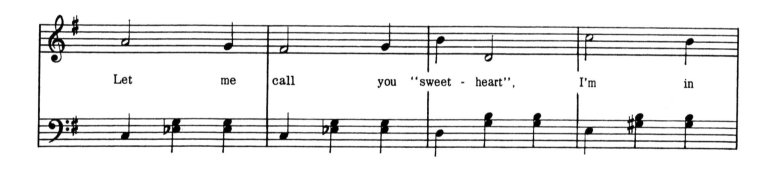

Let   me   call   you ''sweet - heart'',   I'm   in

love   with   you. _____

46 Memories

GUS KAHN

EGBERT VAN ALSTYNE

Mem - o - ries, Mem - o - ries,

dreams of love so true, _____

O'er the sea of mem - o - ries, I'm

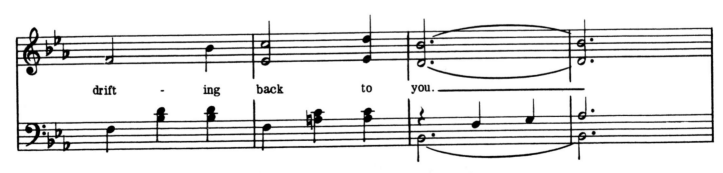

drift - ing back to you. _____

Child - hood days, wild - wood days, A -

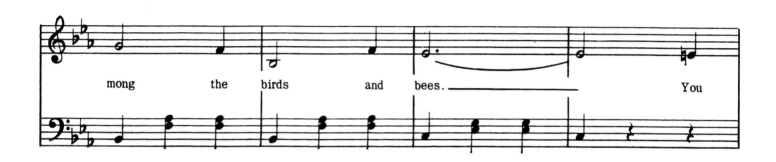

mong the birds and bees. _____ You

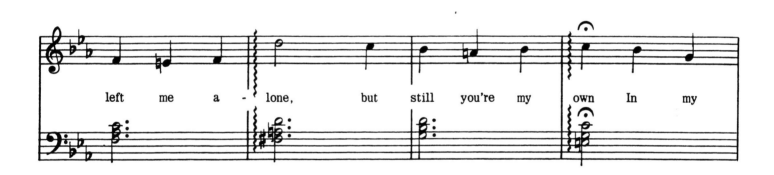

left me a - lone, but still you're my own In my

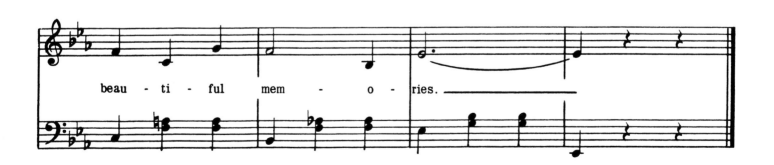

beau - ti - ful mem - o - ries. _____

47 Love's Old Sweet Song

J.L. MOLLOY

1. Once in the dear dead days be-yond re-call When on the world the
2. Ev - en to-day we hear love's song of yore, Deep in our hearts it

mists be-gan to fall, Out of the dreams that rose in hap-py throng,
swells for - ev -er -more Foot-steps may fal - ter, wear-y grow the way,

Low to our hearts, love sang an old sweet song; And in the dusk, where
Still we can hear it at the close of day, So till the end, when

fell the fire - light gleam, Soft - ly it wove it -self in - to our dream.
life's dim shad - ows fall, Love will be found the sweet -est song of all.

CHORUS

Just a song at twi - light, when the lights are low,

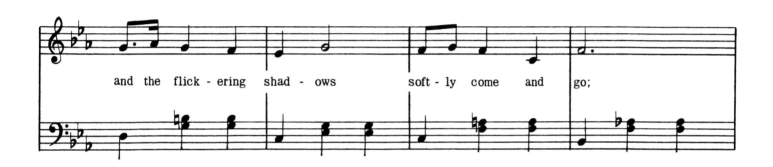

and the flick - ering shad - ows soft - ly come and go;

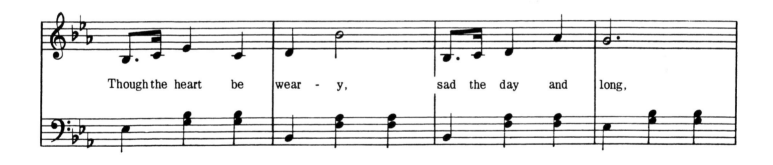

Though the heart be wear - y, sad the day and long,

Still to us at twi - light comes love's old song, Comes love's_ old_ sweet song.

48 Let a Smile Be Your Umberella

IRVING KAHAL, FRANCIS WHEELER and SAMMY FAIN

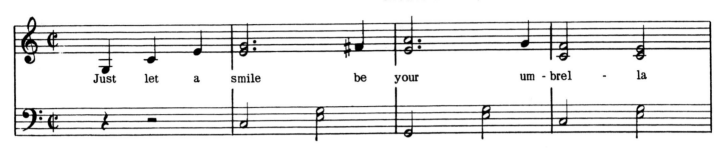

Just let a smile be your um - brel - la

On a rain - y, rain - y day,

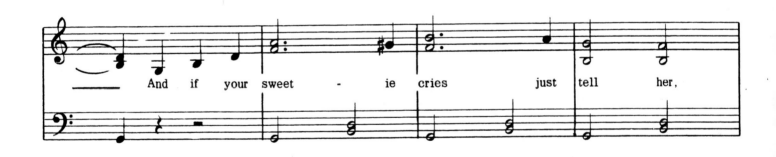

And if your sweet - ie cries just tell her,

That a smile will al - ways pay.

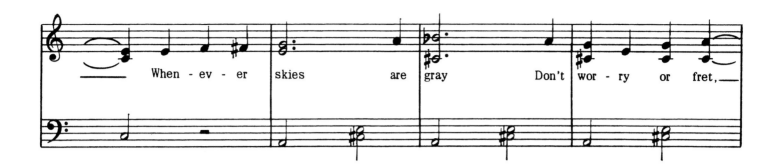

When - ev - er skies are gray Don't wor - ry or fret,___

A smile will bring the sun - shine And you'll nev - er get wet.___

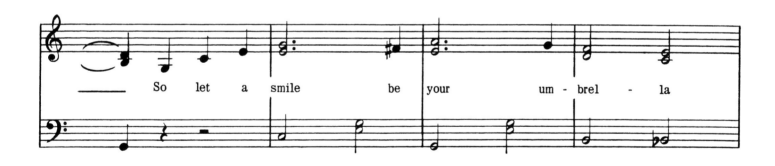

So let a smile be your um - brel - la

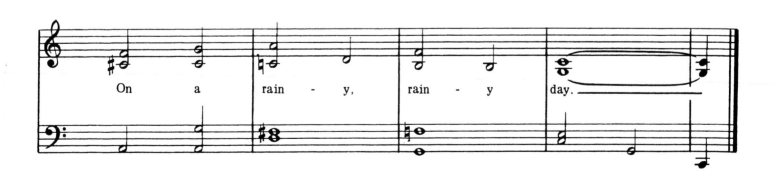

On a rain - y, rain - y day.___

Meet Me in St. Louis

Additional lyrics by TIMOTHY GRAY

Words and Music by ANDREW B. STERLING & KERRY MILLS

Meet me in Saint Lou - is, Lou - is,

Meet me at the fair, _____

Don't tell me the lights are shin - ing

An - y place but there. _____ We will

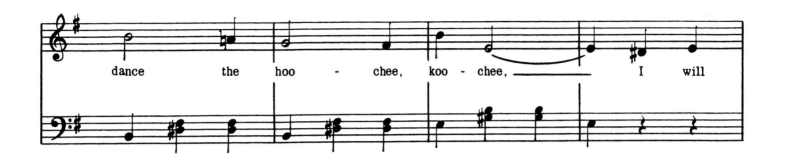

dance the hoo - chee, koo - chee, _____ I will

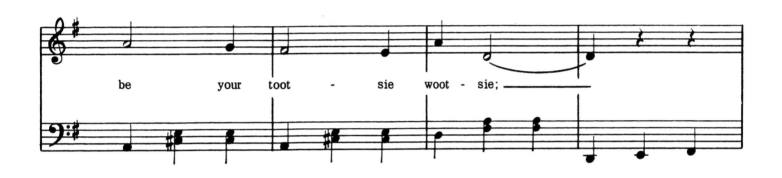

be your toot - sie woot - sie; _____

Meet me in Saint Lou - is, Lou - is,

Meet me at the fair. _____

50 Cruising Down the River

EILY BEADELL and NELL TOLLERTON

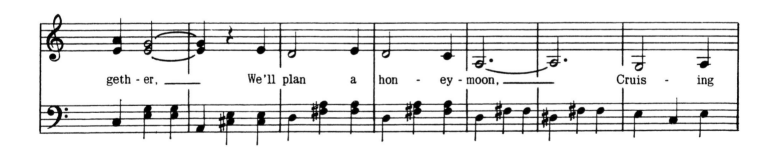

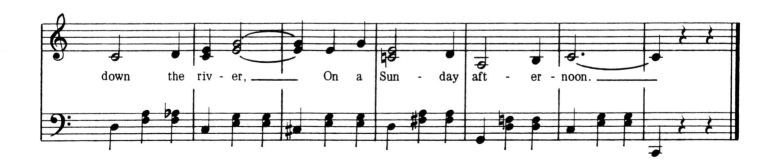

51 Drink to Me Only with Thine Eyes

BEN JOHNSON

OLD ENGLISH AIR

Drink to me on - ly with thine eyes. And I will pledge with

mine, Or leave a kiss with - in the cup And

I'll not ask for wine; The thirst that from the

soul doth rise Doth ask a drink div - ine;

But might I of love's nec - tar sip I would not change for thine.

Keep the Home Fires Burning

LENA GUILBERT FORD

IVOR NOVELLO

53　I Wonder What's Become of Sally

JACK YELLEN

MILTON AGER

Old time pals and old time gals, Where are your smiles to-

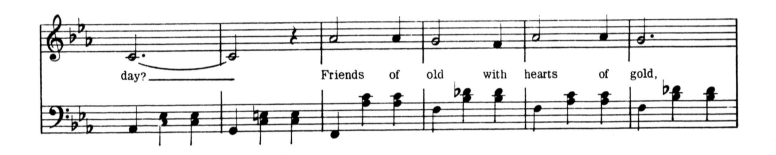

day?_____ Friends of old with hearts of gold,

Where have you drift-ed a - way?_____ Where is John - ny and Mar - y, and

all the rest? And where is the one I love best?_____

CHORUS

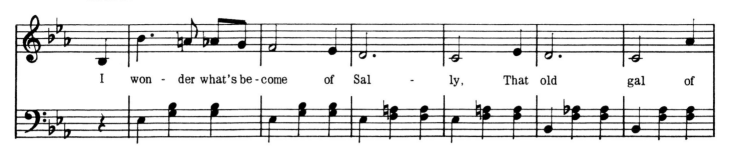

I won - der what's be - come of Sal - ly, That old gal of

mine? _____ The sun - shine's mis - sing from our al - ley,

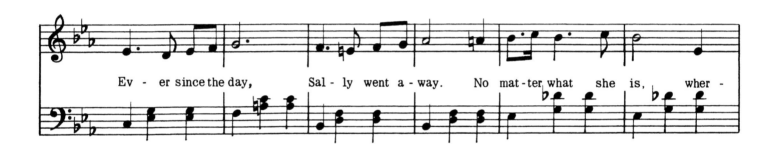

Ev - er since the day, Sal - ly went a - way. No mat - ter what she is, wher -

ev - er she may be, If no one wants her now, please send her home to me. I'll

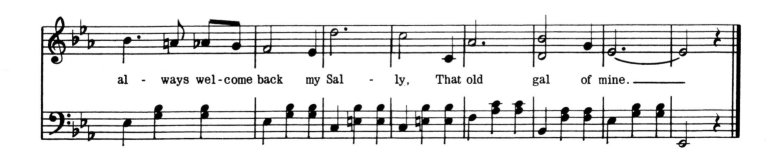

al - ways wel - come back my Sal - ly, That old gal of mine. _____

54   Dixie

DANIEL D. EMMETT

DANIEL D. EMMETT
Adapted from Paul Hill's arrangement

I wish I was in _ the _ land of cot - ton, Old times there are

not for-got-ten, Look a - way! Look a - way! Look a - way! Dix - ie

Land! In Dix - ie Land_ where_ I was born In earl - y on one

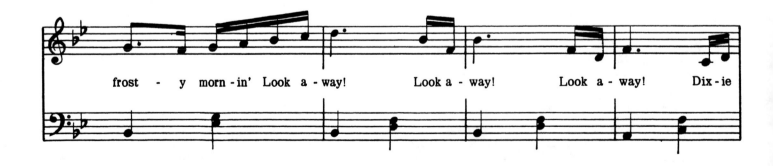

frost - y morn -in' Look a - way! Look a - way! Look a - way! Dix -ie

land! Then I wish I was in Dix - ie, Hoo -

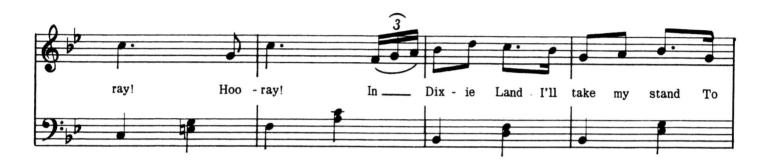

ray! Hoo - ray! In Dix - ie Land I'll take my stand To

live and die in Dix - ie, A - way, a - way, a -

way down south in Dix - ie! A - way, a -

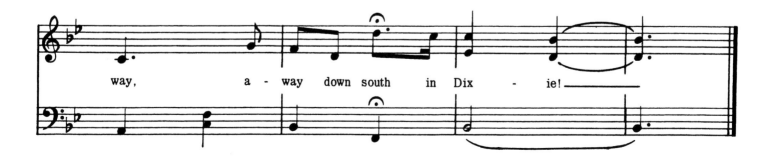

way, a - way down south in Dix - ie!

55   After the Ball

CHARLES K. HARRIS

Aft - er the ball is ov - er,

Aft - er the break of morn, _____

Aft - er the danc - ers' leav - ing,

Aft - er the stars are gone; _____

Man - y a heart is ach - ing,

If you could read them all,_____

Man - y the hopes that have van - ished

Aft - er the ball._____

56 Cuddle Up a Little Closer

OTTO HARBACH

KARL JOSCHNA

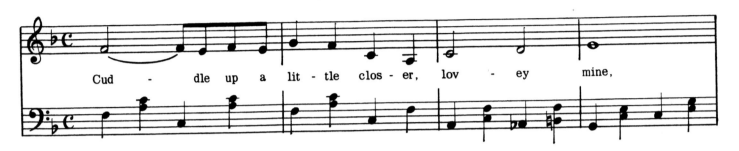

Cud - dle up a lit - tle clos - er, lov - ey mine,

Cud - dle up and be my lit - tle cling - ing vine.

Like to feel your cheek so ro - sy, Like to keep you com - fy, co - zy

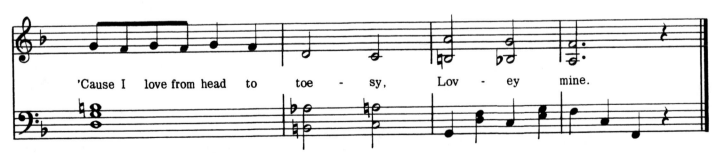

'Cause I love from head to toe - sy, Lov - ey mine.

57 Carolina in the Morning

GUS KAHN

WALTER DONALDSON

58

Ain't We Got Fun

GUS KAHN and RAYMOND B. EGAN

RICHARD A. WHITING

Ev - 'ry morn - in', ev - 'ry eve - nin', Ain't we got fun?

Not much mon - ey, oh! but hon - ey, Ain't we got fun?

The rent's un - paid dear, _____ we haven't a car,

But an - y - way, dear, _____ we'll stay as we are,

Ev - en if we owe the groc - er Don't we have fun?

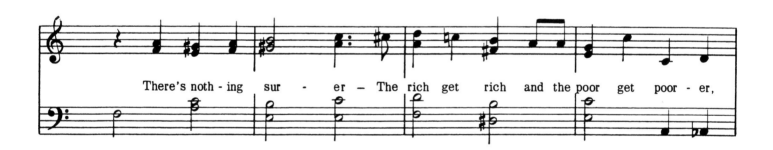

Tax col - lect - or's get - ting clos - er, Still we have fun!

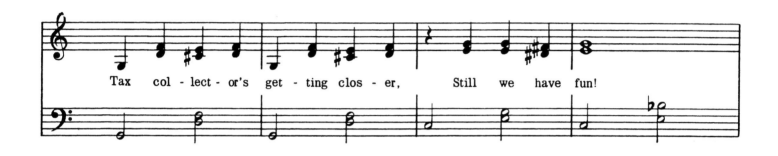

There's noth - ing sur - er — The rich get rich and the poor get poor - er,

In the mean-time, in - be -tween time Ain't we got fun?

59   Let the Rest of the World Go By

J. KEIRN BRENNAN

ERNEST R. BALL

With some - one like you,   a   pal   good and

true,   I'd   like   to   leave   it   all   be - hind   and go and

find   Some   place   that's   known   to   God   a -

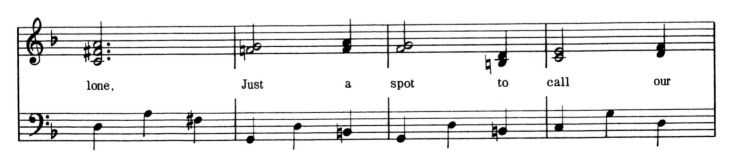

lone,   Just   a   spot   to   call   our

own, We'll find per‑fect peace, Where joys nev‑er

cease Out there be‑neath a kind ‑ ly sky, —————

———— We'll build a sweet lit ‑ tle nest some ‑ where in the

west And let the rest of the world go by. —————

60 Did You Ever See a Dream Walking

MACK GORDON

HARRY REVEL

61 There is a Tavern in the Town

ADAPTED FROM AN OLD CORNISH FOLKSONG

There is   a   tav - ern in the   town,   in   the

town,   And there   my dear love sits him down,   sits him

down _____ And drinks   his   wine   mid   laugh - ter

free,   And nev -   er, nev - er thinks of   me. _____

CHORUS

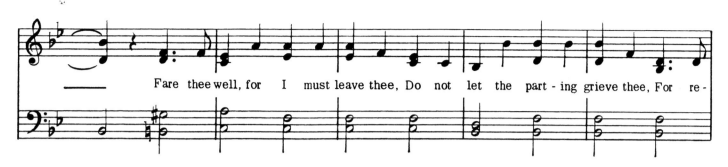

Fare thee well, for I must leave thee, Do not let the part - ing grieve thee, For re -

mem - ber that the best of friends must part, must part, A - dieu,, a -

dieu, kind friends, a - dieu, a - dieu, a - dieu, I can no long - er stay with

you, stay with you, _____ I'll hang my harp on a weep - ing will - ow

tree, And may the world go well with thee. _____

62   If You Knew Susie

B.G. SYLVA and JOSEPH MEYER

If you knew Su - sie Like I know

Su - sie - Oh! Oh! Oh! What a gal!

There's none so clas - sy As this fair

las - sie - Oh! Oh! Ho - ly Mos - es!

CHORUS

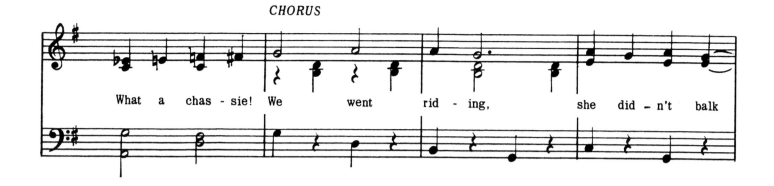

What a chas - sie! We went rid - ing, she did - n't balk

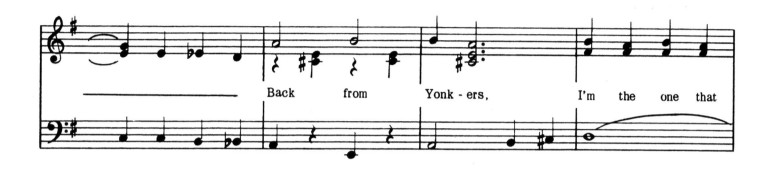

Back from Yonk - ers, I'm the one that

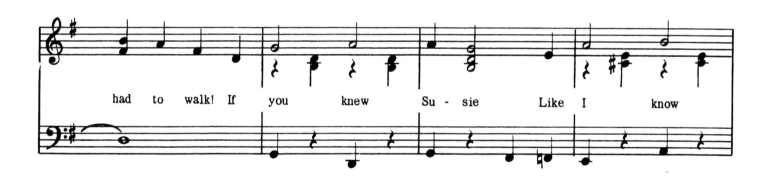

had to walk! If you knew Su - sie Like I know

Su - sie — Oh! Oh! What a gal! _____

2. If you knew Susie
    Like I know Susie —
    Oh! Oh- Oh! What a gal!
    She wears long tresses
    And nice tight dresses
    Oh! Oh! What a future she possesses!
    (CHORUS)

63   In the Good Old Summertime

REN SHIELDS

GEORGE EVANS

In the good old sum - mer - time, _____ In the

good old sum - mer - time, _____

Strol - ling through the sha - dy lanes,

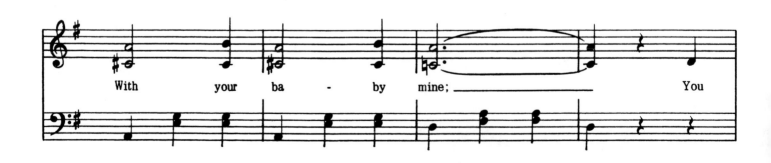

With your ba - by mine; _____ You

hold   her   hand   and   she   holds   yours ,   And

that's   a   ve - ry   good   sign, _____   That

she's   your   toot - sey   woot - sey   In   the

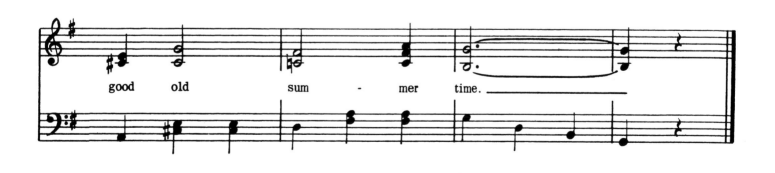

good   old   sum - mer   time. _____

64 I'm Looking Over a Four Leaf Clover

MORT DIXON

HARRY WOODS

I'm look - ing ov - er a four leaf clov - er, That

I ov - er - looked be - fore, _____

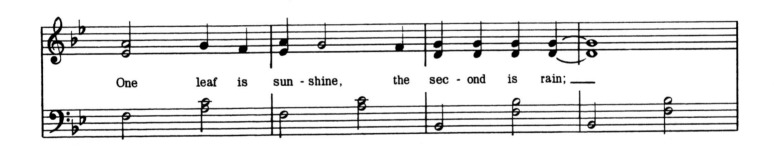

One leaf is sun - shine, the sec - ond is rain; ___

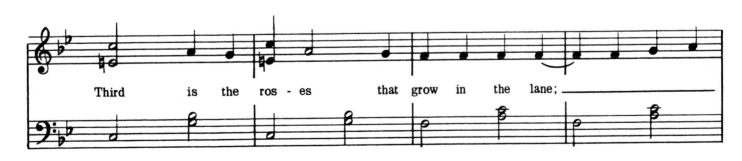

Third is the ros - es that grow in the lane; _____

No   need ex - plain - ing   the one   re - main - ing,   Is

some - bod - y I   a - dore. _____

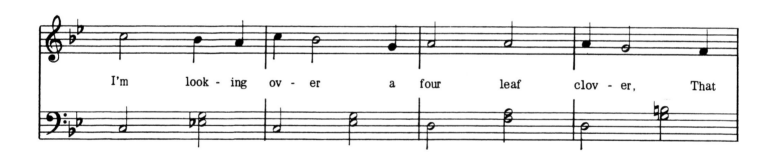

I'm   look - ing ov - er   a   four   leaf   clov - er,   That

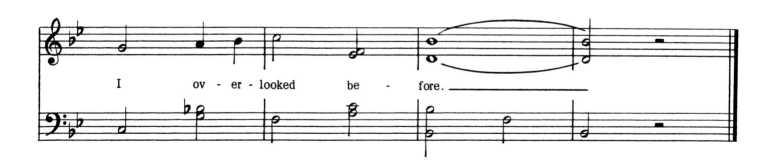

I   ov - er - looked be - fore. _____

65   I Want a Girl

WILLIAM DILLON

HARRY VON TILZER

good old-fash-ioned girl with heart so true,

One who loves no-bod-y else but you;

I want a girl just like the girl that

mar - ried dear old Dad._____

66 Wait Till the Sun Shines Nellie

ANDREW B. STERLING

HARRY VON TILZER

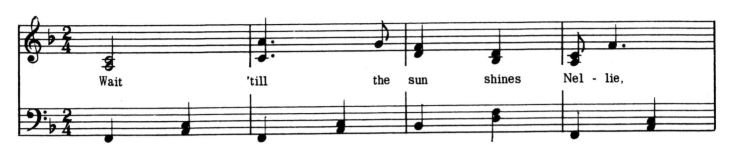

Wait 'till the sun shines Nel - lie,

And the clouds go drift - ing by,

We will be hap - py, Nel - lie,

Don't you sigh, _____

Down   Lov -   er's Lane   we'll   wan - der,

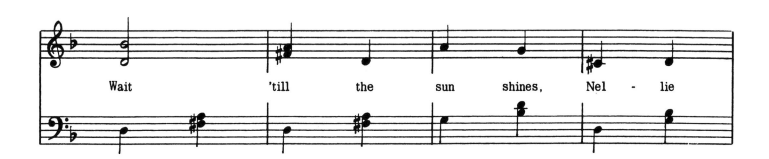

Sweet - heart,   you   and   I, _____

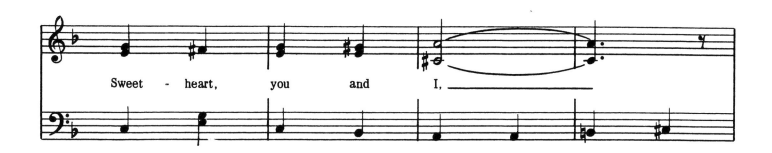

Wait   'till   the   sun   shines,   Nel -   lie

Bye   and   bye. _____

67   Daisy, Daisy

HARRY DACRE

Dais - y,   Dais - y,

Give me your ans - wer do; _____

I'm   half   craz   y

all   for   the   love   of   you, _____   It

won't be a styl - ish mar - riage, _____ I

can't af - ford a car - riage; _____ But

you'll look sweet up - on the seat Of a

bi - cy - cle built for two. _____

Chester, Chester, Here is my answer true:

I'm not crazy all for the love of you.

It must be a stylish marriage,

You must afford a carriage;

For I'll be d .... if I'll be crammed

On a bicycle built for two.

68　When You Wore a Tulip

JACK MAHONEY

PERCY WENRICH

When you wore a tu - lip, A sweet yel - low

tu - lip: And I wore a big red rose;

When you car - essed me, 'Twas then heav - en

blessed me, What a bles - sing no one knows,

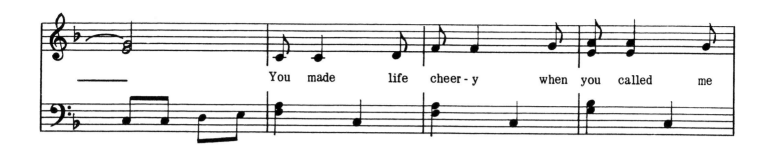

You made life cheer-y when you called me

Dear - ie; 'Twas down where the blue grass grows;

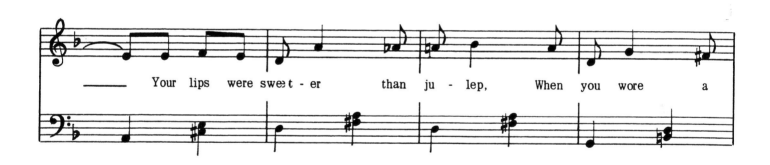

Your lips were sweet - er than ju - lep, When you wore a

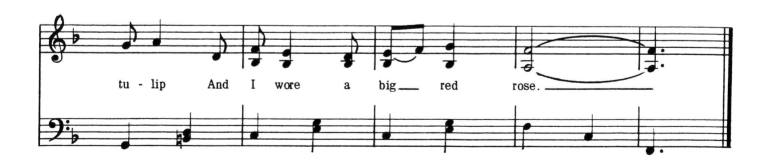

tu - lip And I wore a big red rose.

69   School Days

WILL COBB and GUS EDWARDS

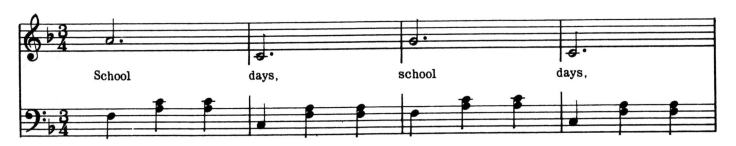

School   days,   school   days,

dear   old   gold - en   rule   days;

Read - in' and rit - in' and 'rith - me - tic,

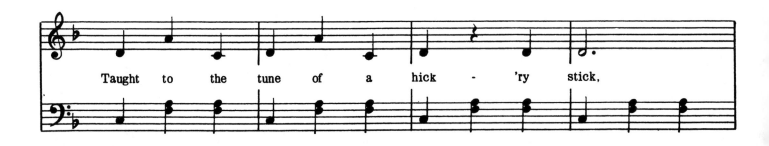

Taught   to   the   tune   of   a   hick - 'ry   stick,

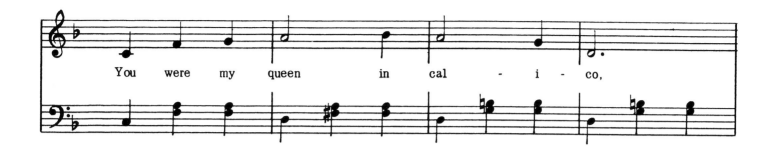

You were my queen in cal - i - co,

I was your bash - ful bare - foot beau, And you

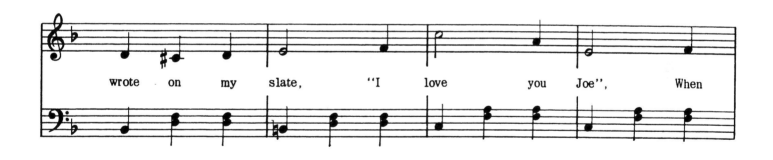

wrote on my slate, "I love you Joe", When

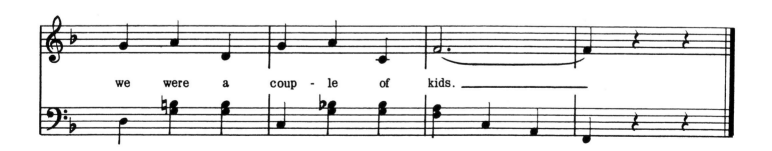

we were a coup - le of kids. _____

71 Way Down Upon the Swanee River

S. C. F.

STEPHEN C. FOSTER

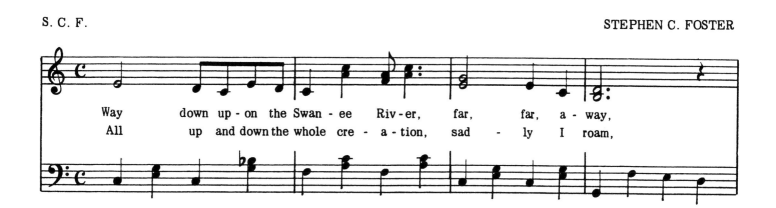

Way down up-on the Swan-ee Riv-er, far, far, a-way,
All up and down the whole cre-a-tion, sad-ly I roam,

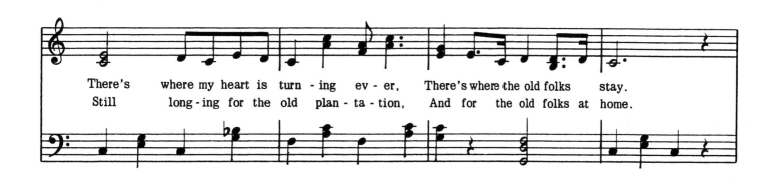

There's where my heart is turn-ing ev-er, There's where the old folks stay.
Still long-ing for the old plan-ta-tion, And for the old folks at home.

CHORUS

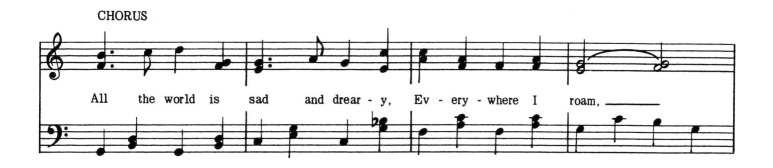

All the world is sad and drear-y, Ev-ery-where I roam,

Oh! Dark-ies, how my heart grows wear-y, Far from the old folks at home.

72 You Are My Sunshine

JIMMIE DAVIS and CHARLES MITCHELL

1. The oth - er night, dear, _____ As I lay sleep - ing, _____
2. I'll al - ways love you _____ and make you hap - py _____

_____ I dreamt I held you in my arms, _____
_____ If you will on - ly love me too, _____

_____ When I a - woke, dear, _____ I was mis - tak - en _____
_____ But if you leave me _____ to love a - noth - er _____

_____ And I hung my head and cried. _____
_____ You'll re - gret it all some day. _____

CHORUS

You are my sun - shine, _____ my on - ly sun - shine, _____

_____ You make me hap - py, _____ when skies are gray, _____

_____ You'll nev - er know dear, _____ how much I love you, _____

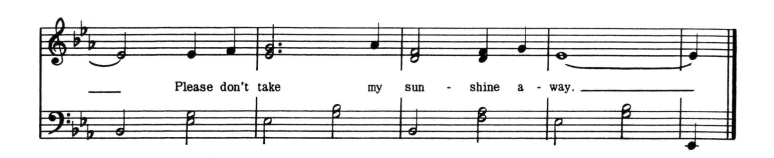

_____ Please don't take my sun - shine a - way. _____

73   Sidewalks of New York

CHAS. B. LAWLOR

JAMES W. BLAKE

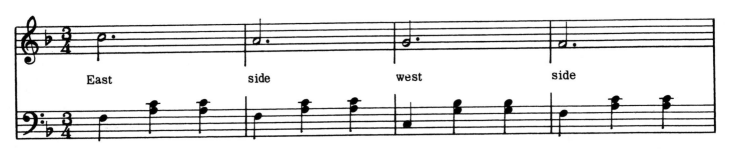

East   side   west   side

all   a - round   the   town, _____   The

tots   sang   "Ring   a - round   Ros - ie"   "Lon -   don

Bridge   is   Fall   -   ing   Down"_____

Courtesy of the publisher, Shawnee Press, Inc., Delaware Water Gap, Pa. 18327

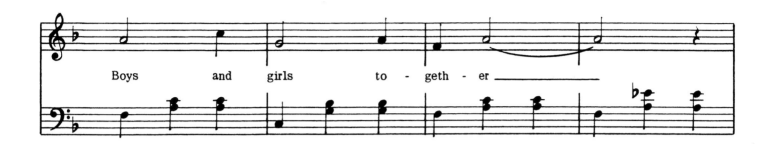

Boys and girls to - geth - er _____

Me and Ma - mie O - 'Rorke _____

Tripped the light ____ fan - tas - tic On the

side - walks of New York. _____

74

Mary

G.M.C.

GEORGE M. COHAN

For it was Mar — y, Mar — y, Plain as an - y name can be; _____ But with pro - pri - e - ty, so - ci - e - ty, We'll say Mar - ie; _____ For it was Mar — y, Mar — y, Long be - fore the fash - ions came; _____ And there is some - thing there That sounds so square; It's a grand old name. _____

By the Light of the Silvery Moon 75

EDWARD MADDEN

GUS EDWARDS

76 Sunny Side Up

B.G. DESYLVA, LEW BROWN and RAY HENDERSON

Keep your sun - ny side up! up!

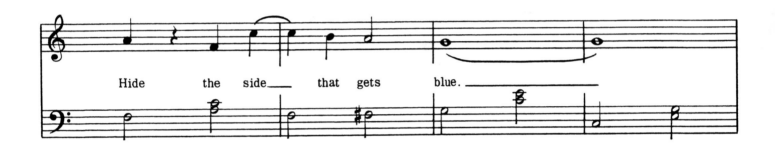

Hide the side___ that gets blue.___

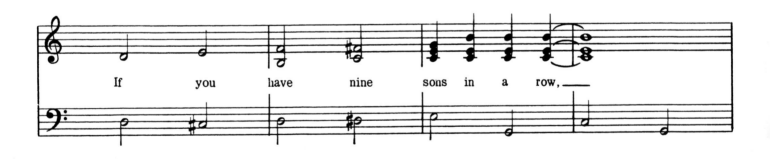

If you have nine sons in a row,___

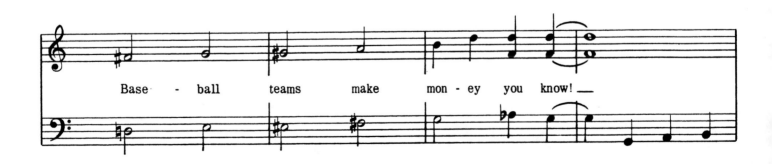

Base - ball teams make mon - ey you know! __

Keep your fun - ny side up! up!

Let your laugh - ter come thru' do!

Stand up - on___ your legs, Be like two___ fried eggs,

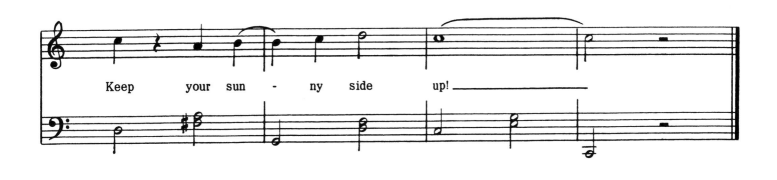

Keep your sun - ny side up! _____

77 Beautiful Dreamer

S. C. F.

STEPHEN C. FOSTER

Beau -ti - ful dream — er, wake un - to me,

Star - light and dew - drops are wait - ing for thee;

Sounds of the rude world heard in the day,

Lulled by the moon - light, have all passed a - way.

78 Bill Bailey, Won't You Please Come Home

H. C.

HUGHIE CANNON

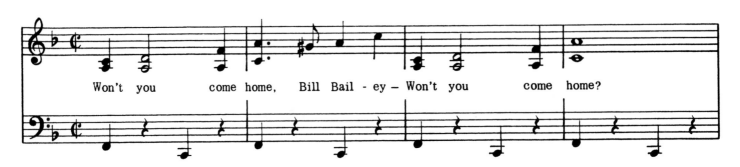

Won't you come home, Bill Bail - ey — Won't you come home?

She moans the whole day long, _____

I'll do the cook - ing, hon - ey, I'll pay the rent,

I know I've done you wrong. _____

Courtesy of the publisher, Shawnee Press, Inc., Delaware Water Gap, Pa. 18327

Re - mem - ber that rain - y eve - ning I threw you out With

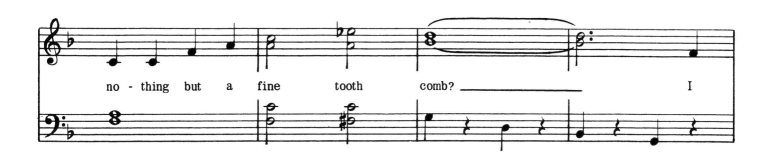

no - thing but a fine tooth comb? _____ I

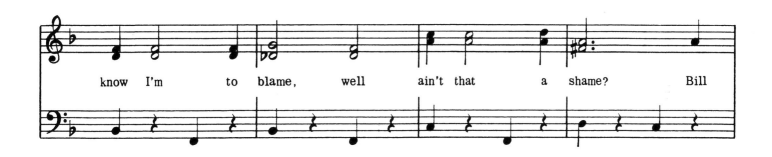

know I'm to blame, well ain't that a shame? Bill

Bail - ey, won't you please come home? _____

79

Let the Sunshine In

S.H.

STUART HAMBLEN

So let the sun - shine in, face it with a

grin, Smil - ers nev - er lose, and frown - ers nev - er

win, So let the sun - shine in, face it with a

grin, Op - en up your heart and let the sun - shine in!

When You and I Were Young Maggie

80

GEORGE W. JOHNSON

J.A. BUTTERFIELD

I wan - dered to - day to the hill, Mag - gie, To watch the scene be -

low. The creek and the old creak - ing mill, Mag - gie, As

we used to long, long a - go. The green grove is gone from the

hill, Mag - gie, Where first the dais - ies __ sprung! The

creek - ing old mill is __ still, Mag - gie, Since you and __ I were __ young. __

81

Nellie Gray

B. R. HANDY

There's a low green valley on the old Ken-tuck-y shore, There I've

whiled man-y hap-py hours a-way, A -

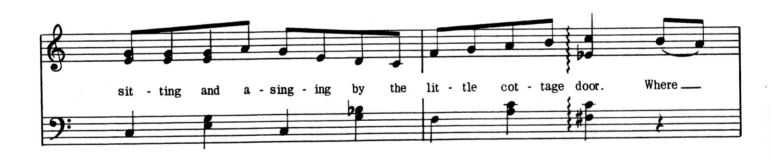

sit-ting and a-sing-ing by the lit-tle cot-tage door. Where

lived my darl-ing Nel-lie Gray, Oh

my poor Nel - lie Gray, They have tak - en you a - way, And I'll

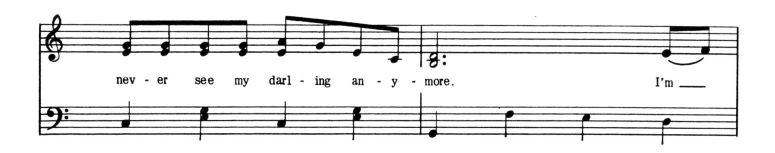

nev - er see my darl - ing an - y - more. I'm ___

sit - ting by the riv - er And I'm weep - ing all the day, For you've

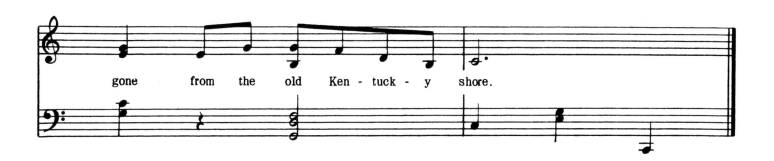

gone from the old Ken - tuck - y shore.

82   I'm Forever Blowing Bubbles

JAAN KENBROVIN and JOHN WILLIAM KELLETTE

I'm   for - ev - er blow - ing bub - bles, _____

Pret - ty bub - bles in   the   air. _____

They   fly   so   high,   near - ly reach the   sky

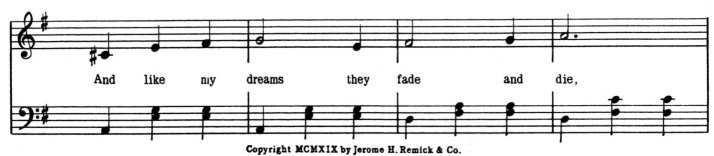

And   like   my   dreams   they   fade   and   die,

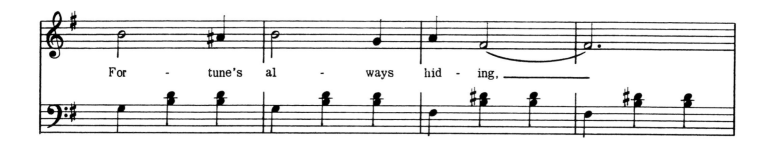

For - tune's al - ways hid - ing, _____

I've looked ev - ery - where, _____

I'm for - ev - er blow - ing bub - bles, _____ Pret - ty

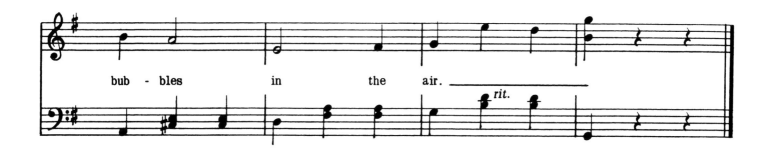

bub - bles in the air. _____ *rit.*

83   The Old Spinning Wheel

BILLY HILL

There's an old spin-ning wheel in the par-lor,_____ Spin-ning

dreams of the long, long a-go,_____ Spin-ning

dreams of an old-fash-ioned gar-den_____ And a

maid with her old-fash-ioned beau._____ Some-times it

seems that I can hear her in the twi - light _____ At the

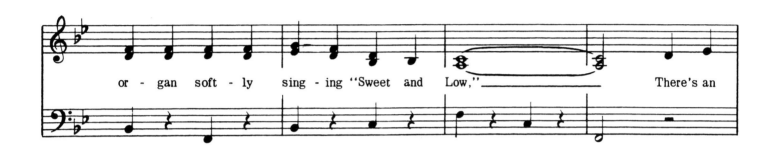

or - gan soft - ly sing - ing "Sweet and Low," _____ There's an

old spin - ning wheel in the par - lor, _____ Spin - ning

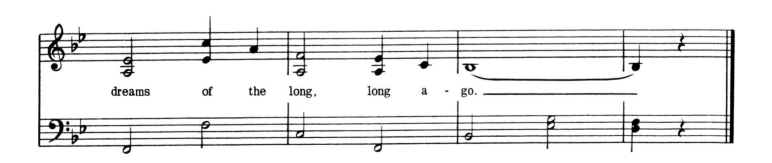

dreams of the long, long a - go. _____

84   Baby Face

BENNY DAVIS and HARRY AKST

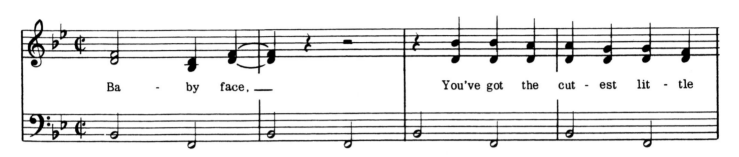

Ba - by face, ___   You've got the cut - est lit - tle

ba - by face. ___   There's not an - oth - er one can

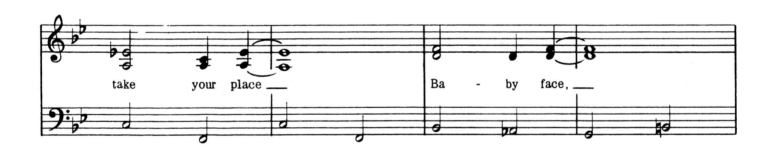

take   your place ___   Ba - by face, ___

My   poor heart ___ is jump - in' You sure have start - ed some - thin'

Ba - by face, ___ I'm up in Heav - en when I'm

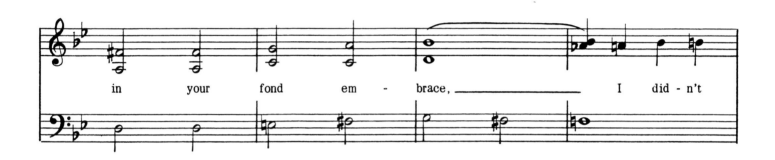

in your fond em - brace, _____ I did - n't

need a shove, __ 'Cause I just fell in love ___ With your

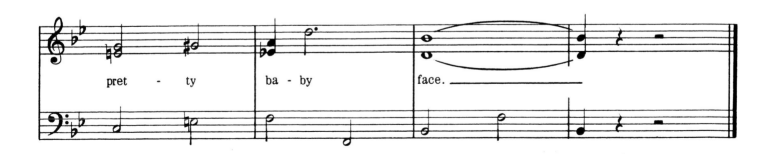

pret - ty ba - by face. _____

85 Back Home in Indiana

BALLARD MACDONALD

JAMES F. HANLEY

Back home a - gain in In - di - an - a, And it seems that I can

see The gleam - ing can - dle light, Still shin - ing bright Through the

sy - ca - mores for me. The new mown hay lends all its

fra - grance Through the fields I used to roam When I

dream a - bout the moon-light on the Wa - bash Then I long for my In - di - an - a home.

Darktown Strutters' Ball

SHELTON BROOKS

I'll be down to get you in a tax - i hon-ey Bet-ter be read - y 'bout

half - past eight __ Now Dear - ie don't be late __ I want to be there when the

band starts play-in' Re - mem - ber when we get there hon-ey The two steps I'm gon - na

have them all ___ Goin' to dance out both my shoes __ When they play them Jel - ly Roll

Blues To - mor - row night __ at the Dark-town Strut-ters' Ball. ___

87 Down By the Old Mill Stream

TELL TAYLOR

Down by the old mill stream, _____

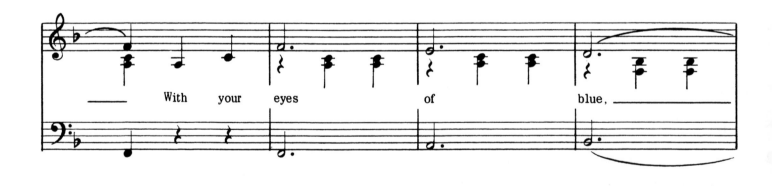

_____ Where I first met you, _____

_____ With your eyes of blue, _____

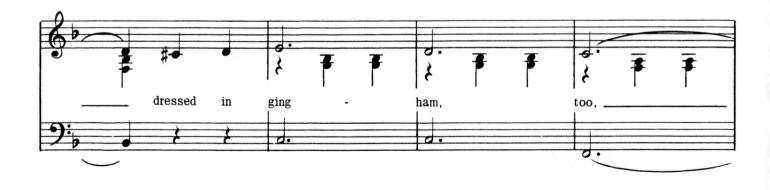

_____ dressed in ging - ham, too, _____

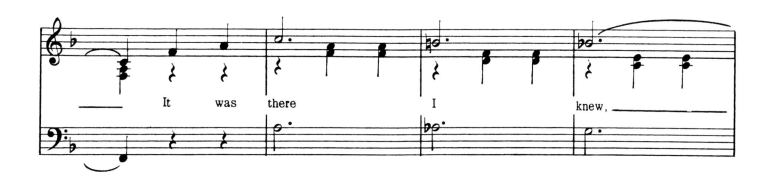

It was there I knew, _____

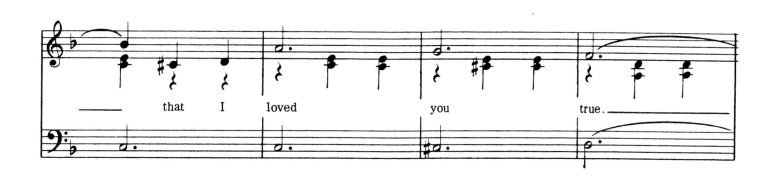

_____ that I loved you true. _____

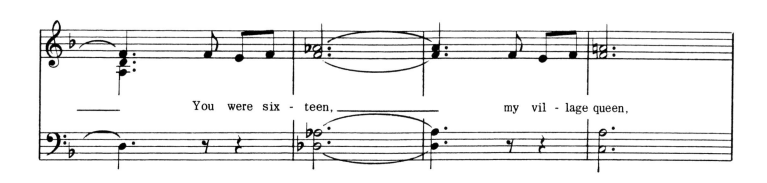

_____ You were six - teen, _____ my vil - lage queen,

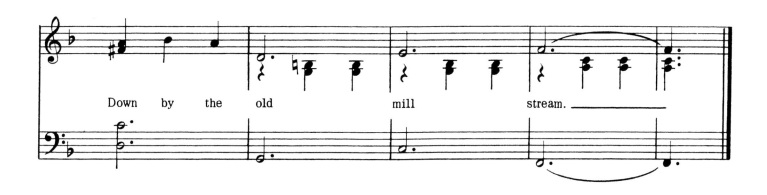

Down by the old mill stream. _____

Index